Father's Day

Oliver Marshall

SUMMER PALACE PRESS

First published in 2005 by

Summer Palace Press
Cladnageeragh, Kilbeg, Kilcar, County Donegal, Ireland

Printed by Nicholson & Bass Ltd.

A catalogue record for this book is available
from the British Library

ISBN   0   9544752   9   1

This book is printed on elemental chlorine-free paper

for
Emily and Claire
and in memory of my mother and father

Acknowledgments

Some of the poems in this book have previously appeared in: *Salmon* (1989); *New Irish Writing* (1986); *Muinteoir Naisiunta* (journal of the Irish National Teachers' Organisation) (1988); *Irish Times* (August 1984); *Rostrum* (journal of the Association of Principals and Vice-Principals of Community and Comprehensive Schools) (1987); *Irish Arts Review* (1987); *The Stinging Fly* (2003); *Cyphers* (no. 55, 2003) and *Black Mountain Review* (2003).

'Uncles' was published as a prize-winning entry in the *Clonmel Nationalist* (1984).

Some of these poems appeared in *Trio 6*, an anthology of new and emerging poets published by Blackstaff Press, Belfast (1990).

Biographical Note

Oliver Marshall graduated from University College, Dublin, with a First Class Honours Degree in Modern English and American Literature and an MA in Modern English and American Literature. He has had three radio plays broadcast by RTE, and has had a poem short-listed for the RTE National Poetry Competition (2001). He has read his work at the Bray Arts Club, the Irish Writers' Centre in Dublin, the Castletownbeare Arts Festival and the Irish-American Society in New York. As a member of the Wildeside Quartet, he had a reading tour in Wales, concluding at the Dylan Thomas Cultural Centre in Swansea. Oliver Marshall worked at the Oscar Wilde Autumn School in Bray, where he edited the literary magazine, *Wildeside*.

CONTENTS

Uncles

in memory of Francis and Christopher Marshall, drowned on a
Clonmel Post Office outing to Clonea, August 5th, 1951.

I never saw you drown.
All my childhood you smiled from the wall like saints,
your faces flushed by the photographer's rouge.
Frankie and Christy. But for the sadness, the names
could have chimed well on a billboard over the Oisín,
or tucked under ten-shilling notes in birthday cards
to relations you never saw.

Drowned at Clonea, August 5th, 1951 …
Sunday after Sunday until I was twelve
I wiped the bird-shit from your gravestone,
or knelt bare-kneed beside my father,
uncertain whether to pray to you or for you;
guilty that in secret I was glad
you, not he, were dead.

I had a hold of their hands, Oliver, only a wave …
But for a grand aunt I would have missed the funeral,
though I remember only black coats, faces, silence.
Not one word was spoken on the way
over or on the way back, my mother said; but
it is easy to imagine the grief: young
trees summery on The Mall, a twelve foot grave.

I have to look at a map to remember the way:
Newcastle, Clogheen, the Vee … At Melleray
you stand for your last photograph. You look happy.
Back in the bus, I imagine you up front, laughing,
or wondering (townies) if the yellow fields were oats or barley,
or counting the days to your wedding (Christy) or the Final (Frankie),
but maybe you sat like my parents, unspeaking, at the back.

Beyond Dungarvan, you lean out to clean your heads
of place-names that every day cling like dust to your
black uniforms: Marlfield, Mountain Lodge, Scrouthea …
Then, flashing like a knife in the sun, Clonea.
You are too long dead for me to mourn,
and now I no longer pray. But I can hold
you here undrowned forever, hands

lifted in my father's hands, above the waves.

Les Derniers Hivers d'un Ancien Acteur des Paroles
for Philip Larkin

Alone in a house whose rooms
of sepia resemble
tombs in an Italian cemetery –
his grandfather, sitting in the first
car in Tipperary, his parents,
smiling in their wedding suits
a year before the War – he thinks for the millionth time
of Pavese's last despairing cry:
Non scrivero più.

Each morning, depression
sits like a pigeon on his head;
he tries to make it lift; it
sits deeper, now a crown of thorns.
In the garden, final roses drop
their heads in crimson and vermilion coincidence;
a child's trike waits like a lost
suitcase for its owner; and high
above a neighbour's roof, ghostly poplars

shimmer like a woman's tresses
in a summer river. Words,
always the same – *father, mother,*
childhood, love – begin like tumours in his brain,
or fester like worms in a fisherman's cup.
It would take a surgeon's scalpel
years to cut them free.
He walks from room to room.
Sentences lie on chairs

like unfinished knitting: *In 1957,*
at the age of nine, I pick
windfalls with my father
in a dying garden. Our fingers touch …
Four years later, in my mother's
pink hand-mirror, I search anxiously
for my whiskered, androgynous face …
At night he dreams
he is the boy Mozart,

all Europe – Paris, Mannheim, Wien –
minueting like toys
to the tinkling of his holy hands;
but wakes instead to find
his own hands crossed, as if
old Nurse Hunt has parachuted in from childhood
to prepare his last (unanointed) evening.
He rises, dons the brown
dressing-gown, that (hooded)

makes him look like Friedrich's Monk.
He tries to write (or shit words); fails.
Falling asleep, he dreams
in hate the moon
is a mad Gestapo searchlight
tormenting the ruins of his once-beautiful
eighteenth-century city. Once, too,
words came like birds from his sleeve.
Now, old artificer, stauncher, *maestro delle belle parole,*
he has forgotten how.

Finches

My father caught finches when he was a child.
In the wild afternoons of winter, he put lime
and a decoy finch on the branches of nearly naked
trees. There was no danger in it or anything like that.
Just the lime, the trees in the winter cold,
the branches still and empty
under a sky of impending snow.

He said he once saw goldfish in a pool
near the Taj Mahal, when he was only five.
He told me that when he was already old.
There seemed no reason to doubt him,
just as when he said he delivered the post
on Christmas Day, 1937, bringing letters
from Coventry, like white stars
out of a darkening sky.

Once he said he saw a burial at sea,
somewhere south of the Bay of Biscay.
I can imagine the brown makeshift box
sliding between the rails of the unsteady ship,
the held candles not lighting in the wind,
the afternoon light swinging like a silver stethoscope
in everyone's faces, my father held up to see it,
in someone else's arms.

It is always winter when I remember my father
and the Christmas he was born, long before
he told me how he trapped the unsuspecting finches
as they came in like small aeroplanes to land
on the innocent-looking lime.
I never suspected then how much he loved me.

But it is the finches I most remember
this last December of the century,
and my father barely eight in the Christmas
of 1914, when the sky was like a white handkerchief
with soon-to-fall snow. That was the War
when they declared a truce for a day.
Everyone ate turkey. And troops
stopped going to Heaven, like misdelivered letters,
or stars falling the wrong way around.

Lecce Remembered

I stood all night in the corridor
of the train from Parma. The river
was completely frozen over. The cathedral
had been a cold shell of disappointment,
dark bricks confidently ascending to nowhere.
It made me worry whether God existed.

In the crowded corridor of the *rapido*
the metal strip on the window forbade me
to lean my head out. *Vietato sporgersi
dal finestrino.* I put my head out, fearlessly,
to test the Italian darkness, wondering
what would happen, still worrying

whether God existed. Nothing happened
but the beauty. I was like a child again at home
with my father, going to matches. Ancona went past,
its soccer pitch flooded by moonlight. Loreto. Bari.
The stations were like a crescendo of racing commas
that blossomed into a full sentence when Lecce

and its amphitheatre came up. The morning resembled
an Italian girl holding out a bottle
of unopened wine. All winter, until summer
came like a white tree, I taught English to people
who couldn't understand me. An Italian girl
fell in love with me. I couldn't respond,

too young to understand that love does not
require two people to speak the same language.
On dark nights, I hung around churches, dying
of homesickness. Even the Latin did not console
me. One night, I rang my father. He answered
the phone in a next-door grocery shop. He must
have stumbled over glass-lidded boxes of Kimberley
and Marietta biscuits to talk to me.

Thousands of Christmas trees and cribs
with lighted candles in windows were brightening
Ireland. But I could not see them. A thousand miles
away, as he re-cradled the phone, I heard my father say:

Lovely to hear your voice.

Music Lessons

I was fourteen when I played my first arpeggio,
but I had been playing the piano long before that.
When I was seven, my red-faced grand aunt
drove in from Fethard to reprimand my mother:

Would you not get that child to play the piano?
So I began with the scale of C major,
my pale boyish hands nervously sinking
into notes that were hard as bone.

My music teacher smoked Woodbine cigarettes.
The ash dropped from her mouth like soft lead
from a small pencil. It burnt the notes,
and it nearly burnt me.

I played scale after scale, thinking
in my mind I was Rachmaninov,
and that the Albert Hall lay before me,
white spotlights picking out my curly head.

I could never please her. Impatient with my playing,
she sent me out to do messages.
I bought country butter for four shillings a pound
and acid batteries for her radio.

She erected a plaque to her dead cat in the garden,
putting me off cats for years. One afternoon I knocked.
She didn't answer. She had died suddenly
the Saturday before. My father bought the piano,

and became angry when I couldn't perform
to his satisfaction. *After all the money we spent*
on you, he said. I closed the lid,
and cried for days. I never saw my music teacher dead.

Someone else must have called the ambulance.
Someone else must have seen one of her hands
dropping over the sides of the blanketed stretcher,
her palm cascading like a sheet of music in the wind.

Memories of Mesen

inspired by the International Peace and Reconciliation Ceremony
at Mesen in Belgium

My father joined the local Defence Force
during the Second World War.
That was the War when Ireland was neutral.
We took down the signposts at wind-tormented crossroads,
hoping the Germans wouldn't find their way
through the small countryside.
At night we turned on wireless sets,
and listened to Lord Haw Haw calling:
Germany calling, Germany calling.

My father went on summer camp from Tipperary
to Youghal. He fell in thistled fields, firing at nobody.
Later, he queued in khaki-coloured tents
for roast beef and stewed apple with thickish custard.
Men in young green uniforms tracked the coast off Dungarvan
for German submarines, and in the evening
listened to the wireless calling:
Germany calling, Germany calling.

My uncle went down, all hands on deck,
on a passenger ship, into a merciful sea.
He survived to die in a car accident in Germany
a year after the War was over. My father
stowed his service medals in cotton wool.
My aunt collected her widow's pension.
The roast beef and custard was better by then.
And peace came back to Europe
like a Volkswagen that has never crashed.

Eighty thousand Irishmen died in the First World War.
I can hear them
falling in the thistled fields at Mesen,
or stumbling to the tops of hills, singing
It's a long way to Tipperary.

Passengers to Faranaleen

I remember a small station
a few stops beyond Fethard
on the Thurles line. Geraniums
in boxes. A signal-shed,
hands a vivid green, now a falling red.
Nothing much else. My father
on the other side of the carriage,
silently totting up the happiness in his marriage,
wondering who would be substitute
for the out-of-action left full back.
Fantastic stars, Berenice and Betelgeuse,
ignoring us, above the long long track.

Me with my mother on the same train,
without my father. My mother in a blue blouse.
Fields going past, lanes leading to the whites
of farms. Men swaying from hayricks supported
by ladders. The two of us, listening to the wheels.
As we passed the Wilderness, my mother
peeled an orange and said
the wheels were saying: *I can I will, I can I will.*
When we passed Fethard and the high wood,
my mother ate the orange, pips and all,
said the wheels were saying:
I knew I could. I knew I could.

My brother married a woman who said *Yes*
to him, a few stops up that line. They must have found
life's best yes in the hedges
between Thurles and Faranaleen, in that green
summer of 1964, when I was sixteen
years old, and was still dreaming of the track
that ran under Berenice and Betelgeuse,
past the Wilderness, past Laffansbridge
and Killenaule, to the geraniums on the window-sills,
and the nothing else of Faranaleen.

An uncle paid two-and-sixpence
to join his fiancée on that train
he thought would never stop coming
by the sidings of Faranaleen. She woke
me from sleep one evening –
I was dreaming of a grand aunt
dead in Kensal Green –
to tell me love was for the forever.
But I could see she was already regretting
the promises she had made
in the corridor of the train
between Thurles and the blue lilac
of my mother's blouse,
and the nothing else of Faranaleen.

Three Days' Darkness

to John McGahern

When I was seven,
The Irish Catholic
said that Heaven
and its apocalyptic
joys were on their way:
three days' darkness
would squat like stray
tenants on the fastness
of our holy land.
Penance would fill the hours
to stay the stern hand
of God above the fires
of Hell. Candles would refuse
to burn in the homes
of mortal sinners or Jews –
thus we'd know the names
of those bound for the far
side of Christ. I kissed
my medals and scapulars,
afraid I had missed
Heaven by my silly
act: in Doctor Murphy's garden
I pulled down the frilly
knickers of a maiden,
and swooned in polymorphous
and oh yes intense
joy on the amorphous
miniature kiss
of a future mayoress.

Heaven never came,
despite the stress
of waiting. The game
of eschatology
was easily revealed
for the codology
it was. Congealed
lives flowed again
along familiar rivers
of dull routine. Rain
fell like unwanted slivers
of sanctifying grace
on sun-forgotten summers
in laurelled Brighton Place.
Busby-headed drummers
led Patrick's Day parades
– there were accordion-chested
mummers, childish escapades
in Troy's tree-infested
shades – but not the long
procession past our sill
to join the black throng
of travellers on Gallows Hill:
Clonmel's bleeding vein
of nightly emigration.
The nearest I ever came
to divine salvation
was when my father,
his arms akimbo,
told my mother
he'd located Limbo

on our small Pye
electric wireless
– I heard the souls cry
in darkness that was fireless –
or when with Jackie Ahearne
I ran down to greet
Sputnik 1 as it turned
the corner of Queen Street,
tacking close to Heaven,
on 5th October, 1957.

Joe

You came each year for Christmas,
sleigh-riding through Wexford and Waterford
like a second-class Santa Claus on the old *Rosslare*.
My mother's only brother.

My father is hardly at the Convent Bridge,
parcels hanging like turkeys from the handlebars
of his black Post Office bike, as I rise
and carefully stow my dreams under a pillow
Persil-white as the hills in my window,
and runwalk Gallows Hill to meet the train,
dropping size five wellington prints
like litter in the ankle-high snow.

In the winter-dark station where
my grandfather queued for the First World War,
a single red light burns – the signal.
It is like a country chapel waiting for a funeral:
taximen stamp their feet like undertakers,
cough Craven A, Sweet Afton and Woodbine coughs,
speculate how much the Fishguard boat is late.
Go home out of that, you friggin' Arab,
one shouts for a laugh,
spotting my queer-shaped, bilious-coloured plastic raincap.
Blushing, I furl my frightened snail antennae
and weigh myself in hundredweights –
or climb the iron bridge to peep
through its Meccano-set bars
on Clonmel lying on for second sleep –
until the red light turns to green,
and the lighted carriages feed like rapid cinematic images
before my timid astigmatic eyes.

Hello, Oliver.
I turn to see you stand,
an apparition in steamsmoke, holding out your hand;
then sit behind you on the cushioned back
of Bernie Keane's black Hackney,
gliding like King Faisal through hankywhite air:
the Railway to 2 Queen Street,
a huge five-shilling fare.

Your suitcase opens like Ali Baba's cave,
dazzling my impatient after-breakfast gaze:
photographs (black-and-white Ilford 120) of the Coronation,
air displays flying like fireworks
over pompous Elizabethan days; autographs:
Gene Autry, Sir Edmund Hillary, Max Bygraves …
for a small-town child, it was a magnificent bazaar,
an anthology of free magician fairs: jars
of Pomade purchased in a Tipperary accent
– *Surely you mean Morgan's Pomaud, sir?* –
the first trousers press in Ireland for my father;
the statue of Eros in miniature; a barometer
I broke by holding to the fire
to see how high the mercury would climb;
chopsticks, dominoes, trick cards, a cricket bat,
and a gasometer-shaped coil of wire
that laboured like a rheumatic cat
down the fifteen steps of our uncarpeted stairs.

You were married in the hot September
of 1959, three days before I was eleven. On
Mill Hill Broadway, in your monkey-suit and thinning hair,
you were like a convert at a First Communion,
a small boy answering the door to love.
Afterwards, you hardly ever came. I remember
a postcard to my mother from Pontin's:
Here for a day on my own. No one else would come …

Last time we met
I drove through the Blackwall Tunnel
with an unhappy wife and a crying child
to Edgware General Hospital, where your own wife
lifts her lollipop like a useless monstrance
over secular London's unending traffic. It
seemed time was a second-hand hat
turned inside out, that
I was the uncle, you the child.

Once this summer, locked like Houdini inside
an ice-thick depression I cannot crack, I said:
I want to end this troubled marriage.
That night you came into the coffin-tight
bedroom of my mobile home, flying
around and around above my head
like a battery-controlled redundant postman,
your empty mailbag
miraculously dispensing love.

Before e-mail Was Invented

My father died before e-mail was invented.
So he never played with the mouse or the mouse button.
He never surfed the internet either.

He was born in 1906, eight years
before the First World War began
and millions died in the muck

at Flanders and the Somme,
while the stars flashed like light bulbs
in the sky, ignoring their suffering.

I heard him speak of the Battle of Ypres,
as if he had been there himself.
Being with my father was like listening to a radio

that was tuned in to history.
He carried his own encyclopaedia of suffering
in his heart. He never booked holidays

by logging-on or logging-off.
He took us to Tramore each year.
I was happy with the ice-cream cones

he bought me, biting them at the ends
so that I could suck the ice-cream into my mouth
like snow to cool me down.

In thirty years on the post,
he must have delivered hundreds of thousands
of letters from people who never heard

of e-mail either. They walked through heather
to places of commemoration and pilgrimage,
or else held picnics on grass that spread out

like a tablecloth. They went to the toilet
near hedges and nettles in fields
splashed with cow dung.

Technology never asked him if he wanted
to save his work. He worked hard all day,
going around like a grocer with envelopes.

At night he lay awake, counting up
how much he needed for next year's holidays.
It kept his mind off his own suffering.

My mother breathed beside him,
thanking God in her dreams for small mercies.
I remember him telling me how the *Graf Spee*

was sunk in the River Plate, somewhere
near Montevideo. It didn't really matter
where Montevideo was, or where the *Graf Spee*

was sunk. His mind was like an atlas,
and I was happy to listen to him,
because I knew his stories were disguised ways

of telling me he loved me.
It rained the day we brought him to the cemetery.
Family, friends, and in-laws put up their umbrellas

before the end, and headed for the hotel,
already thinking of their tea and sandwiches.
I stayed on my own with him to the end.

The coffin went down like the *Graf Spee* into the earth.

Churchill at Harrow

Your father sent you a present of a bicycle
that first year you spent at Harrow.
He was too busy to come and see you himself.
So the bicycle must have been his substitute
for a visit. Politics was too demanding
so it was allowed to get in the way of being your father.
Someone must have bought the bicycle for him in a shop
in Kensington or Chelsea or somewhere like that,
and put it on the train at a West London station
for Harrow, where you mixed with the other boys
in cold dormitories and classrooms and rugby pitches,
not knowing that for you, greatness lay ahead
around the corner of the next century.
The torment of the Luftwaffe. Millions dead.

Your mother seems to have made even more excuses
for not visiting you. She sent a governess instead.
She never lived to see the Second World War.
Your letters still survive in your adolescent hand.
Dear Mama, when are you coming down to see me?
Dear Mama, when are you coming to Harrow to see me?
Harrow, where the railway lines criss-cross each other,
and you cried in the dormitory waiting for your mother.

For most of us suffering does not come in such
giant doses. The day our marriage begins to fail.
The day we realise we were never loved enough,
by our father or our mother.

The King's Shilling
in memoriam FCM d. *1937*

I seem to imagine the whole thing
like the beginning of a Hardy novel:
November 1886. *Fin de siècle* rings
of light loop Kilkenny roofs and hovels
as you set out to take the King's
Shilling. Thirty miles away, Clonmel

waits like a woman for a blind date.
But perhaps it was August, and miles
outside the town you piss into a gate,
while wind skis zigzag through walls
of coffin-coloured corn. Above, fate
shakes open like a scarf: Taj Mahal,

where my father first found his face
in a pool of goldfish; Rawalpindi,
dressed like a bride in rajah lace;
or, a century later, a tiny Sindy
Doll loved by my child in a place
you never saw, Portobello. Dingy

streets near Black Abbey were your
first home. A mother held you
in her shadow. On a table near the parlour
door you wrote in quill: *Mother,*
I'm going to Clonmel. I may never
see you again. Francis. Other

images of flight come, but afraid
to amplify your life with mine,
I plot your journey in my head:
Callan, where you knock nine
pints of cider cleanly dead
like skittles; Killamery; Nine

Mile House, where you fall asleep,
and hear her sad voice cry
Come back, Francis. But you keep
going until church spires rise high
like pencils into Clonmel's deep
red and satsuma-tinted sky.

Sons

You won't be going to school today,
was how my father told me she died.
He stood in my bedroom doorway

holding a tear-damp handkerchief.
His mother. I hardly knew her,
but I understood the grief:

four months before, September,
my own mother was ambulanced away
and hadn't yet come back. I remember

going to see her once, geraniums
tinting the skin-coloured walls
of a now-defunct sanatorium.

I think she smiled and said hello,
but that was all.
It seemed years ago

I followed her in fields above
the town, hoping
for random handfuls of love.

Years later she told my wife
these months from home
were among the happiest of her life.

All winter my father and I kept
mournful company. And now his
own mother was dead, he wept

and pushed me into the black
room where she lay
like Rawalpindi ice-stroked on its back.

I stood in terror, bands
of perspiration breaking out like fire:
I touched her subzero hands.

Two weeks later I didn't care
that she was dead. I knew
my own mother was still there.

I left my father on his own,
and wore my black diamond to see
Gregory Peck in *The Guns of Navarone.*

In the spring, my own mother
came home. Her coat was red, but
her hands were like March weather.

Suitcase

My suitcase stands beside the wardrobe
in my flat. I didn't have it the day
I moved in. I must have had another one
then. I bought my present suitcase
for a holiday abroad. I dragged it behind me
on foreign streets. Midges bit me in my hot hotel.
I picked my way as a sightseer
through full pavements and half-myopic crowds.

I can't remember what I did with the suitcase
I had when I first moved in. I had a lot of books
in boxes which I asked for at the supermarket.
And I had other things, for use in cooking.
I still have the hat and scarf my mother
used to wear. I imagine her putting them on
before the mirror we used to have at home,
before the house was sold. I think of her

combing her hair, or brushing her mouth
with lipstick, before she went down the town
to do shopping. There was a suitcase
in my sister's room. A grand aunt used
it when travelling abroad. There was
a half-scratched-away label on the side
that said *Passenger to Shanghai*.
I cry when I think of the suitcase now,

and the things it once contained.
When I was young, I knelt on the sitting-room chair
and watched families with suitcases
going to England. Some never came back.
My mother went away to hospital
with a small suitcase, not expecting
to be kept long. I wrote letters to her,
stretched out on the floor of the kitchen,

until she came back six months later.
I heaved a blue suitcase across England
and France and down through Italy once.
At the Gare du Nord, I had to put it down
several times, thinking I would never make it.
I kept that suitcase for years afterwards,
not wanting to forget the past,
and that time in Italy when I was

only twenty-two. I don't know if any
grandchild will remember me lugging my suitcase
through Paris, the way I remember my grand aunt
travelling to Shanghai. I don't think
that families are the same any more.
The flat is quiet today. A pale
lemon-coloured light spreads out
from the reading lamp I had to buy

since I came here. It is the coldest
January in Ireland for years. No member
of my family has ever been in my flat.
I don't know if that is because I haven't
asked them, or because they don't want
to come. Next time, I'll pack my belongings
more carefully, dragging my new suitcase
down the steps behind me as I leave.

The Milkman Calling

Twice a week he called to our door,
standing high up in a cart
pulled by a jennet down from the mountains.
The cart swayed so much on the iron wheels

that I thought it would fall apart.
He was too old to get out, so he always
got a passer-by to knock on our door.
I had to interrupt my dinner to go out

and hand him up a cream jug
which he filled with milk ladled
from a churn. All I knew about him
was his name, and that he came

from the mountains. Sometimes the jennet
urinated on the street, before the milkman
flicked the reins on its back, telling
the iron wheels to move away.

I turned aside, not wanting to watch
the yellow water as it flowed down
the channel and into the shore
which my mother swept on rainy afternoons

when it got blocked with leaves. I watched
her from the front room, pressing my face
against the window, as she shovelled
the surplus water into the shore.

I think she strained the milk with muslin,
but not always. It thickened and became lumpy
whenever it turned sour. I buy milk
in the supermarket now, in a plastic carton

that says on the side *ninety-nine point seven
percent fat free*. And, in smaller print:
*The paper used to make this carton
comes from well managed Nordic forests*

where tree growth is greater than tree felling.
In the quiet of afternoons, in this almost neighbourless
neighbourhood, I think of my mother
sweeping the rain and leaves with her scrubbing-brush

to free the shore. I wake at night
to the sound of the milk cart going away.

A Tea Chest of Bunting
to my father

Once a year
my father took home a tea chest of bunting.
It sat like an abandoned birdcage near
the mahogany-stained shelves of silver my golfing
grand aunt won in 1926 Shanghai,
until the night before the Corpus Christi procession.
I held the ladder while he slung them high,
poletop to poletop in a zigzag benediction
of colour, a Dionysian stagecloth of blues, reds, yellows and lime-
greens, a tutti of autumn migrants
congregating two months before their time
to salute the rosary-covered elephant
of the procession, caterpillar with a thousand feet
throatrattling hosanna along the tar-perspiring street.

Each night I write
in my prison-windowed study, self-consciously watching
a moon like a lost Eucharist in flight
between funereal poplars, I think of the tea chest of bunting;
I wish I could snake-charm words from its mouth, fountain-high
in an arpeggio of pizzicato-pink pennants
cat-arching the black-chasubled sky:
ciborium-gold, regatta-red, snow pallor –
I wish all Ireland might queue like communicants
before my kite tails of triangular colour.

Him

Each time he met a new woman
he told himself: *This is the one.*
Women, he found, kept him distant.
It started with his mother.
There was a cot, he remembered,
which he wet with his urine
on nights when a pale moon crossed the sky.
His mother left him there,
listening to his cries.
There were bookshelves beside the cot,
with a red encyclopaedia of gardening
and a book of photographs of the First World War,
with futile rows of guns along the Somme.
He was twelve years old when he read
the memoirs of Beniamino Gigli.

One night, making love to his wife,
doing his best to please her,
she lay back and said: *You are doing all the work.*
The marriage did not last.
From the first night when he struck her
with the flat of his hand across the face
he knew it was not going to last.
The night he knew it was finally over
was the night he said: *I love you.*
And she replied: *But I love you too.*
It was that word *too* that killed him.

On the long strand at Tramore
his father lobbed a tennis-ball.
It landed on the sand and he struck it back.
His father looked at him with those blue eyes
that never expected anything in return.

He woke one February morning
when he was forty-eight years old,
crying because his father was no longer there.
He found on the bookshelves of his single bedsitter,
not a red encyclopaedia of gardening,
not a photograph of the First World War,
but the memoirs of Beniamino Gigli.

Marlborough Road

I lived with you on Marlborough Road,
I came home in the evening to a supper
of omelettes and chips. Afterwards
there was always dessert. One summer

and two winters went by like that.
I played the piano in the evenings.
You corrected copies. A lorry came
one Easter. We packed all our things,

and sat in the back, moving
into the future. I can't remember
when I lost you, and the gift of loving:
then, or there, or some hour

when I began to notice that things
were not going right. Gradations
of time and history are like that.
We move from street to street, kings
and queens of our own happiness,
never knowing our final destination.

The Ghent Altarpiece
to Renée Parsons

You do not begin
with geometric calculation
à l'italienne,
nor with soprano variation
of colour *à l'allemande,*
but with quiet prayer:
Que Dieu m'aide, un flamand,
à achever cette peinture –
then the calm
miniature
scrape of psalmy
colour on the King
of Heaven's cloth,
hear how it sings,
crimson-deep moth.

Citizens of Ghent
swap unhappiness
like so many bent
coins in the darkness
which you illuminate
like a manuscript:
Eve's aberrant
thighs and Pict-
sized genitalia
you easily execute –
simple paraphernalia
of this holy act –
saving, I note,
your most precious oils
for the pendulous weight
of Adam's balls.

Four summers ago
I watched an old man
turn the slow
time-pocked panels
before my agnostic
eyes – now one side,
now another, fantastic
oeuvre of Jan van Eyck
and Hubert his older
brother – and wished I
was less cold
in my faith, that Heaven's sky
could muster a parade
of light to outsummer
this magnificent man-made
sacrament of colour.

For My Daughter Going to Spain

In the blank earliness
of a Sunday morning in Bray,
I pack for you to take away
a photograph of my own parents
on their wedding day. From behind
the framed glass, they smile
in black-and-white towards the camera
in happiness and hope,
looking into a future that contains you and me.

I think of you in your own room
overlooking a garden where an ash tree
grows above a neighbour's wall,
and brilliant fuchsia swings untidily
like a red and purple pendulum
in latish summer. You pack privately
for Spain. Language books.
Blouses. Skirts. Girls' things.
Things I have never seen. Your hands
fold and refold a lightish raincoat

to protect you from the rain.
I have not seen you for eight years.
The silence is like a dark scarf over my eyes.
Inside your head, you carry your own black-and-white
picture of me. More black than white,
I think. I have no real photograph of you at all,
except the pictures of you that jump
like unstoppable newsreel inside my head.

A small child on a Wexford beach. You race
up and down in a red-and-white dotted bathing suit,
then test the summer water with your timid feet.
Or your neat body bends to play
with friendly pigeons in an Italian square,
in hot oppressive air. One afternoon,
in a warm summer before the fuchsia
had sprouted its untidy purple and scarlet flowers,
I clicked the shutter of a twin-lens Reflex camera
F eleven at one-twenty-five, to snap you forever

in a blue bathing pool. Unable to reach you now,
I kiss my mother's face in her wedding-day
photograph. I kiss my father's too.
And think of you, thinking of a future
filled with you and me, as I think of you
thinking of me on the road from Barcelona
to Madrid. On each road you walk,
I walk with you, and I see

in a future bereft of me, my ghost bending down to kiss you
as if in a photograph hidden in deep glass,
your eyes smiling up in hope and happiness at me.

Flight to Manhattan

Another day. I stand at the foot of the bed
in the barely awakened light of a March dawn.
I refold and tidy the red and purple bedcover.

My father will soon be fifteen years dead.
Whenever he spoke to me, I thought the words
came like spoons of silver from his mouth.

He must have stood, often, at the end of a bed
like this, refolding a blanket over the space
he had occupied all night, dreaming, or half-awake,

trying to sort out his own tomorrow.
His days consisted of delivering letters
with expressions of love and loneliness

strewn between the pages like the shapeless
pattern of tea-leaves in a cup. A hard life.
Letters came from London and New York to home,

like birds in summer, and went back the following
spring with shamrock, like green tea-leaves,
placed inside. I remember the American stamps

with the Statue of Liberty looking out at me
like a stone reminder of freedom.
In April I will fly to Manhattan, and look down

on roads and fields never seen by my father
and think of him on country roads delivering
letters with expressions of love and loneliness

from family to family, from friend to friend,
between fields of shamrock and clover,
until fading light and an empty mailbag
told him that this day, too, was over.

Men in Their Fifties

There's something about men in their fifties
that makes me understand
why they can put women off.
Suits. Greying hair.

Rings that seem too obvious
on thickish fingers.
Beer bellies that hang out
when they unbutton their shirts

in pubs, remembering happier times,
or replaying in their minds
moments of vanished passion,
or deceiving themselves about a passion

that never existed at all.
The town was full of men in their fifties
when I was growing up.
They lined up like overgrown schoolboys

in the Corpus Christi procession.
The priest held the monstrance.
As they passed our street, my mother
lit a candle in the window

beside a green vase with lilies of the valley.
At the Main Guard, everyone was silent
as they rang the bells at Benediction.
Not everyone was in their fifties

when I was growing up.
The teachers were usually younger.
Some days they beat the hell out of you.
Some days they smiled and gave you sweets.

I danced in Barry's Hotel when I was fifty,
holding women who were slightly older.
Everyone danced politely in a circle,
looking again for a happiness they once had.

I wake at fifty now,
sometimes at two or three in the morning,
wondering where it has all gone,
wondering what I have done wrong.

I think of the past
because it seems happier than now.
So I keep on trying to go back.
The day I got car sickness

and didn't have to go to school at all.
The evening I came home from the dentist,
and my mother brought me up chips in bed.
I didn't wake in the night then.
I didn't think of the pain of life at all.

Spare Room

We slept in the spare room one night,
just for a change, in the brass bed
we usually kept for friends or family

when they came to stay. You made spaghetti
downstairs on the cooker which had
to be repaired shortly after we bought it.

The oven wouldn't heat properly or something.
Or maybe it was the timer that had gone wrong.
When it was fixed, you used it to make cakes

and meringues thick with cream. You could lick
them with your tongue, before chewing the paper-like
texture that dissolved into white crumbs.

We didn't care about crumbs that night in the spare
bed, the night we had the midnight feast.
Spaghetti, tomato sauce, parmesan cheese.

Two glasses of wine and plates on the one tray.
We were halfway through our marriage,
we were halfway to happiness.

My father stayed in the spare room once
on his own. I could hear him making noise
overhead as we sat in the sitting-room

watching *Don Giovanni* on the small television
I bought one Christmas as a surprise.
I was afraid he was going to fall.

He insisted on coming downstairs to stand
behind me. His mind must have taken it in
somehow, because he pointed at the screen

and said *How is it so good?* I cooked
sausages the other night in a saucepan
as my version of a midnight feast.

I thought of you, and that night, the two of us
content as children over our food.
The brass bed. The carpet. The dresser made of wood.

Silence

Silence seems like my most
constant companion these days. It is always
with me, like a dog at my heels
that I have not yet got used to.

It is there when I wake at night,
when I can't sleep, and have to wait
for daylight to come. My mind
fills with pictures of others then,

as the wind waves like a flag around the roofs.
I fight the emptiness in what way I can.
I see my father rising for the post.
I remember my mother leaning

with her head in her hands, sighing
like the wind over a point not made
in a lost argument. My parents always
seemed to be regretting things,

except the day they exchanged wedding rings.
Love lasted in our house, even though
it was spread on differently for each of us,
like icing on a cake not quite made to perfection.

But they did their best. But they did their best.
I hear the wind cry. *Why can't you leave
these things rest?* I think the day will never arrive.
The present is like a leaking roof

over my head. *Your parents are dead.*
Your parents are dead. I think I'll plant
a tree for them, so that the wood may grow tall
and preserve their memory. Not even the wind

can destroy that. I breathe deeply. Something
has been rescued from the emptiness.
I wash, dress, prepare to face the day now.
Despair goes away. Hope begins to grow.

Saying Goodbye to Mr. Larkin

Suddenly I am sick of it all,
all the years I have devoted to you
and those poems that seemed like small
masterpieces, so beautiful and true.

They helped me face living.
Bedsitters like iceboxes. Healing rain.
Sexual fantasies that keep collapsing.
A rabbit with myxomatosis dying in pain.

To me they were like pictures of a loveliness
that had vanished before it could be attained.
You seemed to be saying that happiness
was not for us. Our lives were confined and stained.

So, here in Hull, at this second conference
on your work, the summer fails to bloom.
Even the trees outside the library lack bounce.
When you died, English poetry went into a room

from which nobody has rescued it since.
Certainly not these academics who treat
you with passionless precision, your beauty becoming the meat
for their self-advancement. I wince

when somebody complains about a full stop
put in the wrong place on the headstone over your grave.
I am miles away from home. I want to take a non-stop
train home to Ireland, where I think I can save

myself from what seems like the unhappiness
of your life, falling like snow in summer
around me. But instead, I book with a cross-
mannered landlady in a hotel near

Princes Avenue. Two beds. Two cups for tea.
Biscuits covered with cellophane for this makeshift
life of mine. Everywhere I go I meet only me.
I take out my diary, push words like drifts

of snow across the page. *Feeling not that good.*
This excoriating pain of loneliness. Silly
expressions. *Sound of axes in an inescapable wood.*
I catch the train to Manchester Picadilly,

changing for Crewe and Holyhead. No porters any more,
just computerised screens that tell you
what platform to stand on. I think of Tramore,
where we went on holidays long before

I ever heard of Philip Larkin, and wonder
if there is still some small child
inside me, looking outside for tender
things. My mother in a white blouse one mild

evening in summer. My father on the beach,
teaching me to swim. My brother and sister
smiling into a box camera. Each
of us not knowing what incoherence the future

would hold. Suitcase. Tennis-rackets stored
away in cupboards for the winter. All those mossy
thoroughfares, before I even knew what poetry was about. A hoard
for my pen to dig in. A grand aunt who was bossy.

Back in Bray, I pick up brochures for my holiday
in Tramore, prepare my diaries for what I know they'll say:
Two biscuits left out in cellophane for me.
All day met nobody. Nobody at all. Nobody but me.

Bird on Putland Road
for Claire

I heard a bird sing this morning in the back garden
of my house on Putland Road.
I did not know its name.
My mother pointed out birds to me when I was a child,
naming them by their feathers and calls.
The wagtail I could recognise by sight, and my ear knew
the warble of the woodpigeon. The swoop of a seagull
I knew, the yellow beak diving and scavenging.
But I did not know this bird's name,
not from its music anyhow.
All I could hear was the song, singing
in the garden on Putland Road.
It was like white music in the young spring morning.
It went on, and on. And then it paused.
Even the pauses were like soft chords of joy,
because they reminded me of you.
They served as a relief to all pain,
like a gold eclipse over seas of distance.
I thought of you, my daughter,
studying alone in the house
where I used to be your father,
your head bowed over books,
diligently, constantly, true.
And I knew, as I heard the bird,
singing louder and louder,
that even though I was not in the house any more
with you, I loved you deeply,
and wished I could always be there with you,
to celebrate whatever rhapsodies of joy
that came your way,
and to ease all hurt, all pain,
my love falling on your head,
like soft notes of rain.

Thinking of My Mother

Sometimes now, these empty afternoons
when I am past fifty, and sit
listening to woodpigeons call or a dog bark,

it is then I remember my mother,
like a reflection on pale water, as if
she was there, and not quite there at all.

That's the way with some and more with others,
I heard her often say. Or, at the end of a night in winter:
Thanks be to God we lived so long, and did

so little harm. One afternoon in childhood,
I found her diary in the small polished table
in the front room, and read what I should not

have read, words never intended for me.
Heart not too good. Feeling bad all day.
I closed the diary and ran away from the suffering,

not knowing that these anxieties would one day
be mine. She never knew how much I loved her.
Telling her, or giving her presents, seemed no use.

On her last birthday, I wrote on the coloured card:
Thank you for being my mother.
She rang me one Sunday evening, and said, quietly:

Thanks for the message. Her voice
had an air of quiet loneliness.
I was past fifty years of age that evening.

But as we spoke across the distance,
I knew then that my efforts to love
my mother had been worth it after all.

Father's Day

I think of you,
just as you were
the last Sunday
we met,

eyes wet
as a child,
hair this way and that
like distraught grass.

What time is Mass?
you ask,
for the one hundredth time,
and Jesus, I can't wait

to get away from the weight
of it all, wishing
I could be
your child again

under huge September moons.
But I stand my ground,
soothe you as best I can.
The afternoon breathes

mayflowers, trees,
a protection of mountains
under a mature sky.
I kiss you goodbye,

drive happily home that same
landscape of black fields
and amber lights strung out
like Post Office twine

not caring that soon
it will be my turn
to stand
in the front line.